SCOTLAND'S COAST

SCOTLAND'S COAST

A photographer's journey

Joe Cornish

HALF TITLE PAGE – *Tràigh Uuige, Lewis, sunset*
FRONTISPIECE – *Low tide, Rackwick bay, Hoy*
TITLE PAGE – *Frosted foreshore, Upper Loch Torridon*
DEDICATION PAGE – *Bay of Laig, Eigg*

Contents

For Jenny, Chloe and Sam.

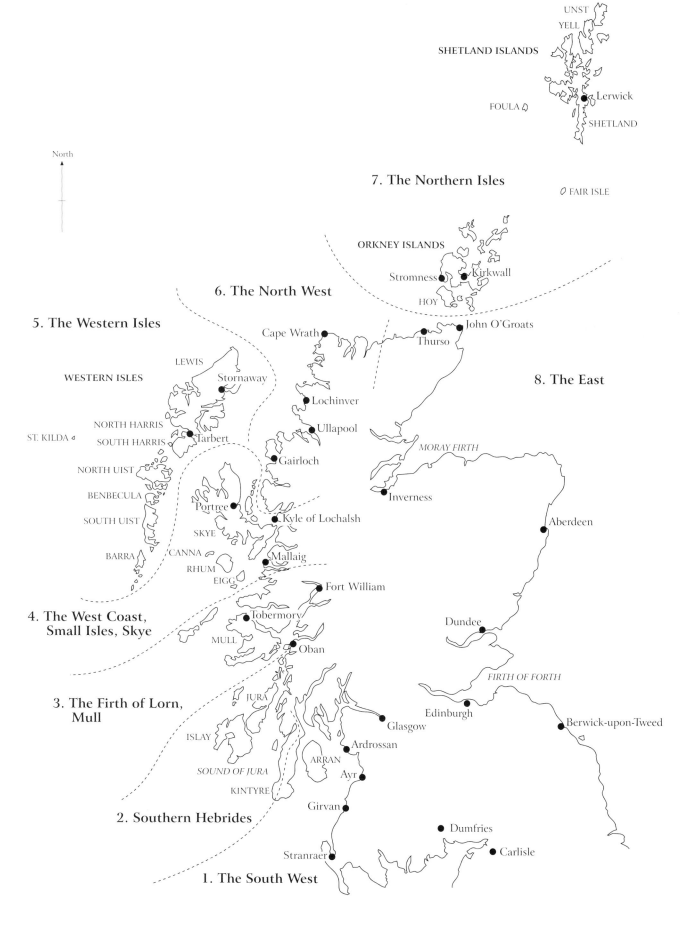

North

SHETLAND ISLANDS

UNST
YELL

FOULA

Lerwick

SHETLAND

7. The Northern Isles

FAIR ISLE

ORKNEY ISLANDS

Stromness   Kirkwall

HOY

6. The North West

5. The Western Isles

Cape Wrath

Thurso

John O'Groats

8. The East

LEWIS

Stornaway

WESTERN ISLES

Lochinver

NORTH HARRIS

ST. KILDA

SOUTH HARRIS

Tarbert

Ullapool

Gairloch

MORAY FIRTH

NORTH UIST

BENBECULA

SOUTH UIST

Portree

Inverness

Aberdeen

Kyle of Lochalsh

SKYE

BARRA

CANNA

RHUM

EIGG

Mallaig

Fort William

4. The West Coast,
Small Isles, Skye

Tobermory

MULL

Oban

Dundee

3. The Firth of Lorn,
Mull

JURA

FIRTH OF FORTH

ISLAY

Glasgow

Edinburgh

Berwick-upon-Tweed

Ardrossan

ARRAN

Ayr

SOUND OF JURA

KINTYRE

Girvan

2. Southern Hebrides

Dumfries

Stranraer

Carlisle

1. The South West

Foreword

Although it is a relatively small country, Scotland has a coastline that would suit a small continent. Totalling 6,214 miles, or almost exactly ten thousand kilometres at the high tide line, it represents 69% of the United Kingdom's total. A piece of string that long would almost reach from Edinburgh to Cape Town. The offshore islands, all 787 of them, and the fantastically fragmented peninsulas and sea lochs of the west coast are largely responsible for this abundance.

How can a photographer even begin to do justice to such a subject in one book? As I travelled around I came to realise that the northern archipelagos, the Western Isles, or indeed all of the major islands would each provide ample material for a complete photographic book. There is enough subject matter here to occupy a creative lifetime, let alone a year or two. The selection process would prove daunting.

Scotland's notorious weather made completing the project to deadline a special challenge. While light of transcendent revelation offers occasional photographic heaven here, lengthy spells of gloomy cloud, wind and rain are far more common. In the time allotted it was inconceivable I could photograph all my chosen subjects in perfect light. I would have to work differently.

One way of adapting to the inevitable was to acknowledge that the 'theatre of light' in which I love to work was not the only valid language for a landscape photographer. When great light occurred, of course, I worked my socks off. When it did not I kept my eyes and mind open, and tackled those subjects that still spoke to me in the quiet voice of soft light.

The large format camera I favour imposed a useful discipline by limiting the range of subjects; although it allows me to explore many creative options, birds, seals or other wildlife subjects are not really among them, except where they are part of the scenery. I also avoided people, architecture (most of the time), and urbanised coastline; these were not part of my mission.

Mostly, I concentrated on the natural beauty of sea and landscape, and the subtle variations of mood, depth and emotion which light can impart. The photographs inevitably include some evidence of human occupation, for Scotland's coast is settled everywhere (although only lightly in the north west). If I responded mainly to inspiration, I also occasionally felt compelled to document the manufactured waste which leaves some high tide marks looking like landfill sites.

There were many highlights for me, and inevitably these were often the occasions when I had the company of friends or family. Experiences shared were experiences doubled as far as I was concerned. But, with or without companions, certain places appealed to my sensibilities more than others, so naturally these predominate in the pages that follow. My passion for boulders meant that I was drawn to beaches with distinctive geology. And white sand beaches seduce me completely. I remember an afternoon at Tràigh Eais on

Barra with a sky that, although weak in sunlight, composed a cloud in my viewfinder that perfectly echoed the stream on the white sandy beach in the foreground. I was so amazed I almost forgot to press the shutter as it drifted into my field of view.

No book of this size can ultimately do more than provide a narrow cross-section of the wonders Scotland's coast has to offer. The Sahara-like dunes of Forvie in the east, and the savage precipices of St Kilda in the far west (shown on these pages) give a sense of its amazing variety. Readers with some favourite beach, or bay, or headland in mind may well be disappointed not to find it featured here, but it would be impossible to go everywhere and see everything.

Six thousand miles may be a long way, but I drove at least three times that distance in the course of making the pictures. The miles in Scotland can seem very long to modern drivers, even those accustomed to the traffic-clogged motorways of England. The roads that lead to the Highlands and Islands are reminiscent of an earlier era of motoring. Although most are in excellent condition, many are still single-track with passing places, and jaywalking sheep as well as the occasional deer can be a real hazard. But even the impatient motorist may find compensation in the regular exchange of smiles, nods and waves that are an essential courtesy at passing places. On Islay I noticed that many motorists raise a hand in acknowledgment to every passing driver, even on two-way roads, a custom that reminded me of the south of Ireland on my first visits there in the early 1970s. It is all part of the Highlands rhythm of life, where the demanding landscape, the weather and the hours of daylight dictate the daily routine.

Although people in southern Britain can drive to Scotland, it is easier, cheaper and quicker for most to fly to many Mediterranean destinations than to drive anywhere north of the Scottish central belt. The physical difficulty of getting there, and the unruly weather make the Highlands a destination for the committed traveller, not for the sun-seeking holiday-maker.

I had some fantastic experiences in a kayak while exploring around Mull. And there's no doubt sailing is a wonderful way to see this coastline, but above all, the coast of Scotland rewards the walker. When I found myself walking there by the sea, whatever the season, the space and solitude set my mind wandering. And as I soaked in the marvels and wonders of the coast I began to think there was little difference between wandering with the feet and wondering with the mind, and in the end it seemed they were just different aspects of the same experience.

I am often asked to name my favourite destinations for photography anywhere in the world. Allowing for my less than comprehensive knowledge of the earth's landscapes, I can say that, for me, at least three or four of those places will be found between the covers of this book. And does one stand out among them? That is for me to know and for you to enjoy finding out!

Greenock

Glasgow

P.17

P.22   Pp.16,   Ardrossan
P.12   18, 19   Irvine
P.11, 23
                  FIRTH
P.21   OF   Ayr
                  CLYDE
ARRAN

KINTYRE   Pp.14, 15

AILSA CRAIG   Girvan

                            Dumfries

Stranraer

                            Carlisle

Pp.13, 20

LOW TIDE
Machrie Bay, Arran

The Golf Coast

A clockwise route around Scotland's coast begins at the border with England – near Gretna – on the Solway Firth. But my own journey really starts at the Mull of Galloway, the headland that marks the far south-west corner of Scotland's mainland. The south west is sunnier than many parts of Scotland, and it is home to some of the world's most famous traditional links golf courses, including Royal Troon and Turnberry.

Overlooking Culzean Bay, just north of Girvan, is one of Scotland's greatest palaces, Culzean Castle, now owned by The National Trust for Scotland; from here there are fine views of the immense basalt island-dome of Ailsa Craig, which dominates this part of the Firth of Clyde. From Ardrossan a ferry serves Arran, an island of such astonishingly varied geology that it is often used for field study work. At 2,876 feet (874m), Goat Fell on Arran is the highest peak in Scotland south of the central belt.

The coastal hinterland of Glasgow is heavily populated and partly industrialised, although distant views of islands and mountains like Ben Lomond are a reminder that the Highlands are only an hour or so away. The western part of this region is framed by the long and isolated peninsula of Kintyre, which forms a stepping stone to the southern Hebrides.

Metamorphic rocks, Torrisdale, Kintyre

13

HIGH CLIFFS
Mull of Galloway

The Gulf Stream ensures a mild climate in western Scotland. Even so I was astonished by the carpet of wild garlic and ferns that I found growing immediately above the shore north of Culzean Castle. This was a habitat I would have associated more with Cornwall than the Firth of Clyde.

Photogenic castles by the sea are a Scottish speciality, much exploited by the tourist industry. Their romantic appearance and historical importance, not to mention cafes and gift shops, are irresistible to visitors, and castle photographs are much in demand for cards, calendars and tins of shortbread. Not wishing to add to the existing surplus of images I had more or less decided that castles would not feature in this book. But I promptly abandoned this firm resolution when I saw Culzean Castle. I just could not help but be impressed by its monumental appearance and dramatic setting. But I decided that, if I made a photograph, it would focus on the environment and include the castle only to show its context. My conscience was clear.

The formidable island-dome of Ailsa Craig rises from the sea to the south west, but on the two days I spent exploring here the air was dense with haze and Ailsa Craig remained infuriatingly out of sight. Forced to turn my attention elsewhere I found myself transfixed by the biological richness of the woods by the shore.

Most west-facing cliffs that I know tend to be wind-scoured and wave-beaten, and colonised by tough, low-growing plants and flowers especially adapted for this demanding ecological niche. But at this southern end of Culzean Bay, in the shelter of the castle headland, woodland thrives. A mixed population of native British broadleaf trees such as oak, ash and birch, along with that burgeoning immigrant, sycamore, shaded a carpet of wild garlic, interspersed with ferns, bluebells, primroses, daisies, saxifrage and other wild flowers. On the beach sandstone is the prevailing rock, although riven by volcanic dykes. Above, Culzean Castle seems to rise straight up from the edge of the cliff. It is an audacious, majestic location, evoking the great castle of Cair Paravel in C.S.Lewis's tales of *Narnia*.

Coastal woodland in spring, Culzean Bay

15

16

ROCKPOOL IN SANDSTONE
Corrie, Arran

ARRAN
From Ardneil Bay

18

Cartographically-speaking, I like to see a ragged coastline with plenty of relief. Headlands and bays, estuaries, islands and stacks offshore, and other coastal features are the visual raw material on which a landscape photographer thrives. For this reason, Arran looked unpromising. Although often described as Scotland in miniature, its simple kidney bean outline on the map bears no resemblance to Scotland's prodigiously torn-up western flanks.

But Arran's charismatic display of geology well and truly compensates. The island's wide variety of landforms bear witness to the fact that it stands on a geological boundary zone where past upheavals have brought together rocks of many ages and kinds, whether igneous, sedimentary or metamorphic.

The shoreline between Corrie and Merkland Point, where visitors stop to watch the local seal population bask on the rocks after a busy night's feeding, is a miniature paradise for the landscape photographer and geologist. The bedrock is red sandstone, formed by desert sands when this part of Scotland lay on the equator 350 million years ago. Although these fossilised dunes are now mostly covered by seaweed, their fabulous cross-bedding planes and projecting fins of harder minerals are still exposed at the top of the tide line. Such rocks can, of course, be found elsewhere in the world, in places like Utah or Jordan, but on Arran they benefit from having the sea as a backdrop. On this spectacular platform lie many formidable granite boulders, erratics that originated from the slopes of Goat Fell, which overlook this part of the coast. These stones were carried here on the glacier that once covered Arran's mountains. I found the juxtaposition of these two contrasting rock types with their utterly different shapes and textures both visually charming and slightly surreal.

The colours of Corrie's sandstone shore have to be seen to be believed. Especially when warmed by the early morning sun, the rock's reds and yellows make a dazzling contrast with the familiar greens of seaweed and the blue of the sky.

Sandstone foreshore, Corrie, Arran

GRANITE ERRATICS
Corrie, Arran

20

Mull of Galloway

LICHEN-COVERED ROCKS
Drumadoon, Arran

22

I expected Arran to be commercialised and busy, sitting as it does in the Firth of Clyde, with an excellent ferry service from Ardrossan. But although it has a thriving population of around 4,700, and many visitors, its island charm remains intact. And in the north and west it has an authentic air of wildness.

South of Machrie on the western side of Arran is the tiny hamlet of Tormore. My visit there coincided with the deepest trough of a spring tide, and some strong winds. The very low tide exposed a foreshore of sand seaward of boulders, and my choice of viewpoint was partly determined by a desire to keep the camera down and out of the wind, as well as by my wish to dramatise the patterns of the rippled sand.

The coast to the north is Machrie Bay, beyond which rise the rounded summits of Beinn Bharrain and its flanking hills. Only a mile to the south is the King's Cave, where, according to local legend, Robert the Bruce had his memorable encounter with a spider; though it is now believed the Bruce's lair was almost certainly on Rathlin Island, off the north coast of Northern Ireland. There are a number of caves and overhangs here, originally carved out of the old red sandstone by the sea. Now they stand high and (relatively) dry above a raised beach formed by isostasy, or the bounce back of land relieved of its burden of glaciers at the end of the Ice Age. A mile further south is Drumadoon, a basalt plateau that was once an Iron Age hill fort. Although it now overlooks nothing more threatening than Shiskine golf course, Drumadoon still seems to dominate a wild, weather-beaten shore when seen from the King's Cave.

Another raised beach fringes the sea north of Machrie where the coast swells west to Imacher Point. At first sight the shoreline here holds no surprises, but closer inspection is rewarding, for it reveals amazing, wave-beaten metamorphic rock formations, another masterpiece in Arran's geological repertoire.

A mile due east of Tormore are the many neolithic sites of Machrie Moor. While Britain does have stone circles and monuments more celebrated than these, it is hard to think of any where the concentration of remains is so extensive or the setting so awe-inspiring.

Contorted metamorphics, Imacher Point, Arran

WINDY DAY
Machrie Bay, Arran

The Southern
Hebrides

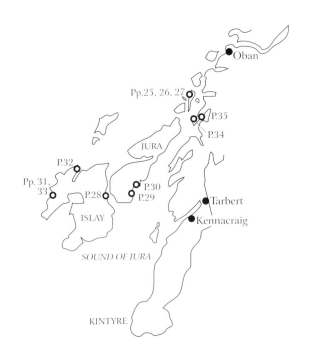

Pp.25, 26, 27

P.35

P.34

JURA

P.32

Pp. 31,
33

P.28

P.30

P.29

Tarbert

Kennacraig

ISLAY

SOUND OF JURA

KINTYRE

Oban

Whisky and whirlpools

Islay and Jura seem to go together as naturally as 'i' precedes 'j' in the alphabet, but in reality these close neighbours are remarkably different. Islay is served by ferries from Kennacraig and Oban, has a population of nearly 4,000, is a major contributor to the British economy as the whisky capital of the world, and was once seat of the Lords of the Isles who ruled over all of the Western Isles. Jura, although closer to the mainland, is served only by a ferry from Port Askaig on Islay. Its mountainous and lonely landscape, dominated by the quartzite Paps of Jura, is home to fewer than 200 people (although there are

6,000 deer) and it is plagued by midgies. However, it does boast a fine distillery at Craighouse.

Between Jura and the small island of Scarba lurks the Corryvreckan, a menacing whirlpool generated by a fierce tidal rip and an undersea stack.

North of the Kintyre peninsula on the mainland is Knappdale. Further north again and close offshore lie more islands, including Seil, whose famous old stone 'Bridge over the Atlantic' spans a narrow channel of seawater. A short ferry crossing links Seil to Luing, once a major quarrying centre, but now largely peaceful.

Sun setting behind Garvellachs, Luing

DECAYING HULL
Luing

Through the straits dividing the islands in this part of Scotland run the most severe tidal overfalls in Britain. Although the Corryvreckan whirlpool is the most notorious, the tide also flows through the Sound of Islay like a river in flood.

For days the Paps of Jura had remained resolutely, demurely wrapped in a duvet of white cloud. Their extra height seemed to guarantee their privacy. But at dawn one morning, as I walked south-east past the Craighouse Pier, the handsome quartzite domes emerged silently in the still air. No early sun split the clouds, no wind disturbed the surface of the water. An ethereal calm prevailed as the sky gradually lightened. The cloudscape thinned and thickened, and a few breaks gave glimpses of the purest blue imaginable. Nothing felt hurried. The young day seemed to be breathing in some slow cadence as mists ebbed and rose around the Paps. By the time I had closed up my wooden field camera, shouldered my tripod and considered breakfast they had once more disappeared.

Wreck of the Wyre Majestic, Bunnahabhain, Sound of Islay

QUIET DAWN
Craighouse harbour

30

FIERCE SHELLS
Loch na Mile, Jura

TIDAL INLET
Machir Bay, Islay

32

CATTLE GRAZING ON DUNES
Loch Gruinart, Islay

DUNE
Machir Bay, Islay

STONE JETTY
Keilmore, Paps of Jura beyond

SEA LOCH SHALLOWS
Midwinter, Loch na Cille

The Firth of Lorn, Mull

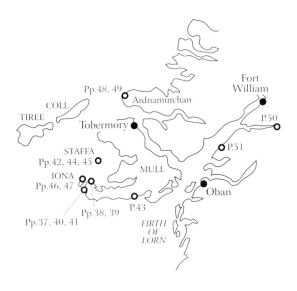

Pp.48, 49

Fort
William

COLL

Ardnamurchan

TIREE

P.50

Tobermory

STAFFA
Pp.42, 44, 45

P.51

IONA
Pp.46, 47

MULL

Oban

Pp.37, 40, 41

Pp.38, 39

P.43

*FIRTH
OF
LORN*

THRIFT GROWING IN GRANITE
Fidden, Mull

North-south divide

Where the Great Glen (nearly) cuts Scotland in two, it meets the sea in the west at the Firth of Lorn. To the south of here, lochs and sea lochs lie roughly on a south and south-westerly axis. Immediately north they run (with a few exceptions) westerly, and in the far north they run north-westerly. Topographically, the whole of the west of Scotland can appear as a fan radiating from some magnetic force deep in the Cairngorm Mountains.

Mull sits in the Firth of Lorn, like a wedge forming the north-south divide. This large island is mainly the product of massive volcanism some 65 million years ago, with big mountains, and soaring basalt cliffs to prove it. Many more islands lie offshore to the west including the Treshnish Isles, Coll and Tiree, which has the sunniest climate in Britain. Of these islands Iona and Staffa are, for different reasons, the most renowned; The National Trust for Scotland owns both.

The busy town of Oban provides ferries to the islands as well as being an important fishing port, and the main market place for this richly varied and serrated coast. Across the Firth of Lorn lies Morvern, north of which is Ardnamurchan, an isolated peninsula. Near to the Point of Ardnamurchan is Sanna Bay with its beach of beautiful white sand.

Abandoned blackhouse, Kintra, Mull

WEATHER OVER BURG AND THE SOUND OF MULL
From Kintra

GRANITE FORESHORE
Fidden, Mull

THRIFT AND GRANITE ISLANDS
Fidden, Mull

42

Although Staffa understandably attracts the attention of tourists, there are numerous other locations on and around Mull that display excellent volcanic rock features. Isolated by huge cliffs, Carsaig Arches are a full four-mile walk from the end of the road, and their sheer remoteness and inaccessibility ensures they are seen only by the dedicated few.

CARSAIG ARCHES
Mull

HEXAGONAL BASALT DETAIL.
Vault of Fingal's Cave, Staffa

My first landing on Staffa was made by kayak, after a voyage through rain, wind and wave. Unfortunately, drizzle and deathly light made that day a non-event photographically. A week later I was able to make the photographs I needed on a sunny day, having got there by tourist launch. But it is the first visit with my paddling companions Steve, Nicky and Ken that I will always remember.

Staffa squats low and dark to the west of Mull, a brooding fortress of vertical rock walls. Although surrounded by a world of islands, it has no near neighbours, as if all potential companions have been frightened off. From a distance Staffa wears an intimidating snarl that seems to say 'come and get me if you think you're hard enough'.

The basalt features here are so geometric, so perfect, that the myth describing the island's construction by a giant seems almost more plausible than the geological reality. How could a chaotic river of molten lava cool and crack into such an orderly matrix of vertical pillars (or perhaps they should be called staves, since Staffa shares the same derivation)? A slow rate of cooling and the molecular structure of the basalts that form the pillared layer appear to be the answer. Further layers of basalt above and below the pillars form pediments and capitals for the columns. Geologists describe the rock in the capping layer as amorphous lava, but it is far from shapeless. Seen close up, it appears to be composed of hundreds of millions of wriggling hexagonal larvae, waiting to grow into fully developed columns.

Although the Great Face is Staffa's most instantly recognisable feature, Clamshell Cave where the ferryboats moor is worth the journey in its own right. Fingal's Cave, immortalised by Mendelssohn's *Hebridean Overture*, takes time to appreciate. The rock is so dark that little light can penetrate the 250 feet (75m) long chamber. Once accustomed to the darkness it is possible to take in the amazing hexagonal honeycomb vault and to tune in to the complex rhythm of sloshes, sighs and swells as the sea ebbs and flows. Like the many who came before and since, Mendelssohn was inspired!

The Great Face, Staffa

FINGAL'S CAVE
Staffa

46

TIDELINE AT TWILIGHT

Iona

WHITE STRAND OF THE MONKS
Iona

The long journey to the western cape of Ardnamurchan leads to
Sanna Bay, described by some as the most beautiful beach in
Scotland. Solitude, space and superb views to the Small Isles fuse
magically here. White sand and smooth rock anticipate the
scenery as you travel further north.

SANNA BAY AND THE SMALL ISLES
Ardnamurchan

DUNE GRASSES

Sanna Bay, Ardnamurchan

Deeply glaciated valleys have allowed the sea to penetrate deep into Scotland's mountainous interior. This produces wonderful photographic (and sailing) opportunities. But it often means driving three times as far as the crow flies.

INLAND SEA

Pap of Glen Coe from Kinlochleven

THREE HORSEMEN
Castle Stalker, Loch Linnhe

The West, Small Isles and Skye

P.66, 67

P.68

Portree

SKYE

Kyle of Lochalsh

Pp.70, 71

CANNA

Pp.62, 63, 65, 69

Pp.59, 61

RHUM

Mallaig

Pp.53, 56, 57, 58, 64

EIGG

P.54

Pp.55, 60

BAY OF LAIG

Eigg

Marvels of nature

Mallaig is the main port for the Small Isles. These rugged islands are still only accessible by foot-passenger ferry, which helps preserve their unique atmosphere. Rùm, the largest, is almost entirely mountainous. Closer to the mainland, and more populated is Eigg, where the islanders set a precedent by collectively purchasing the island in 1997. The National Trust for Scotland owns a third island, Canna. North of Mallaig on the mainland is Knoydart, a mountainous peninsula flanked by Lochs Nevis and Hourn. It is virtually deserted due to the lack of road access.

Skye is arguably Scotland's most famous island, and is now permanently linked to the mainland at Kyle of Lochalsh by the Skye toll bridge. Its outstanding scenery is exemplified by the soaring Cuillin summits and the remarkable rock formations of the Trotternish Ridge. The mainland approaching Skye is heavily visited, especially between Kintail and Kyle of Lochalsh, where the picturesque island fortress of Eilean Donan is a major tourist attraction. North of Kyle of Lochalsh is Plockton, a charming village on the coast where the sea meets Loch Carron.

54

Gravestone and An Sgurr, Eigg

CALM EVENING
Morar

Names have a curious way of influencing our expectations. Before I ever visited them the names Skye, Boreray and Iona gave me a sense of anticipated wonder. But Eigg? According to David Dorward's book, *Scotland's Place-Names*, Eigg means 'notched isle', but to a Sassenach like myself, Eigg is easily confused with the English word egg. Somehow, I just wasn't inspired by an island so named.

So it was almost as an afterthought that I caught the (foot-passenger only) ferry from Mallaig late in October. From the boat I watched the vast plateau of Beinn Bhuide, rising to over 900 feet (300 metres) above sea level, wrap a basalt wall along the eastern face of the island. On arrival at Galmisdale there was no one around to offer a lift, so I walked three miles over to Cleadale on the other side of the island, hoping to catch a ride as I went. But no cars came by. Eigg does not appear to need congestion charges.

Cleadale is a typical island hamlet, an untidy, unself-conscious collection of houses, rotting tractors, rusting cars, tin sheds and abandoned crofts. Yet in such a setting, tidiness must seem trivial, bourgeois. To the east Beinn Bhuide forms a gigantic amphitheatre; if you wanted to stage a play for an audience of titans, this would be a good spot. To the west, two beautiful beaches – Bay of Laig and Camas Sgiotaig, the Singing Sands – divided by a sandstone headland frame a view of Rùm, an island composed almost entirely of mountains.

Eigg has no pylons, no mobile phone masts and, as I discovered, very few cars. Yet satellite TV and broadband internet access is available here, and since the islanders (currently around 85 in number) now own and run their island there is every reason to suppose they will prosper. If commercialised tourism can be avoided, then a quiet, idyllic and sustainable way of life may be preserved.

What's in a name? An Eigg by any other would look as awesome. But it just might attract more visitors.

The afternoon I spent at the Bay of Laig was one of those never-to-be-forgotten occasions when the light just got better and better. By the time I had finished, shouldered my 20kg camera backpack and tripod, and begun my walk south it was twilight, and a full moon lit my way as I trudged happily (and hungrily) back to my B&B.

Limestone nodules, Bay of Laig, Eigg

57

LATE AFTERNOON
Rùm from Bay of Laig, Eigg

58

SANDSTONE SLOT CANYON
Camas Sgiotaig, Eigg

FROST ON SEAWEED
Loch Duich

LATE SUNLIGHT
Mouth of River Morar

61

WINTER AFTERNOON
Five Sisters of Kintail from Loch Duich

62

On Skye, the Cuillin Hills hold lofty dominion over the south of the island; indeed they are the highest of Scotland's island mountains. Arguably the best view of them is across the waters of Loch Scavaig from Elgol. Whatever the weather, the cliffs and shoreline here make wonderful walking territory.

Forests of seaweed offshore produce a lot of waste material, and the top of the tide is marked by lines, sometimes prodigious heaps, of old seaweed. Such natural waste breaks down, decomposes, dries out and eventually returns to the life cycle, either fertilising shoreline habitat as it blows inland, or returning to the seawater as a nutrient.

Occasionally the stench of decaying flesh betrays the presence of a corpse. It may belong to a seal, a bird, or a sheep, or even a goat. All this is part of nature's theatre, of the cycle of life and death. But our manufactured waste is not. Because the high tide concentrates materials at the top of the beach, the coast has become the world's junkyard. Every single beach I explored in Scotland was affected, however remote, wild or isolated.

Shipping is a major source of rubbish. The oceans appear so huge to those who sail them that it must seem ridiculous to think twice before throwing waste overboard. But water is dense stuff; consequently most waste floats. I found a number of beached refrigerators on my travels. Waste doesn't disappear into the ocean, it mostly ends up on beaches.

Plastic floats and buoys, plastic lobster pots, miles of plastic rope and netting, plastic and Styrofoam fish boxes and trays, plastic fuel drums and nylon fishing line all seem to migrate to the top of the tide line, courtesy of the fishing industry. Fishing is a hard, dangerous way to make a living, and fishermen may well feel that their survival is more important than recycling their junk. But I feel nostalgic for the days when rope was made of hemp.

Ironically, marine litter seems to be worse in the more remote spots, perhaps because there are not enough people here to pick over the flotsam and jetsam, or because there are fewer proud locals keeping their beach clean, or because the local council has no funding, or incentive to clean it up. Whatever the reason, the sense of a paradise lost is sometimes very strong.

Sheep skull, Elgol, Skye

CUILLIN FROM ELGOL
Skye

64

SUNLIT STONES
Bay of Laig, Eigg

INCOMING TIDE
Elgol, Skye

66

The remotest western limits of Skye culminate in a lumpy single track road over
Duirinish to Mointeach nan Tarbh. From here there are great views southeast over
Moonen Bay, and southwest to Neist Point with its lighthouse, and gigantic buttress
cliff dropping sheer into the sea. Mointeach nan Tarbh is itself a vast natural fortress
whose high plateau is protected by tiered basalt cliffs.

SUMMER EVENING
Neist Point, Skye

ISOLATED BASALT PILLAR
Mointeach nan Tarbh, Skye

68

It is perhaps stretching the point to say that The Old Man of Storr is part of the coastal landscape. The great rock pillar and its satellites, a landslip detached from the Trotternish ridge, stand over a mile inland. Yet who can deny that, judged from the best vantage points to the north, the Sound of Raasay behind the pinnacles makes the scene? The association with the sea is, therefore, a strong one. Besides, to me a book on Scotland without the Storr is unthinkable! It is a place to which I have been many times, and where I am sure I will continue to return. In my experience there are few landscapes on earth that can match it for atmosphere.

SUMMER DAWN
Old Man of Storr, Trotternish, Skye

SOFT LIGHT, HARD ROCK
Elgol, Skye

70

AFTER RAIN
Summer morning, Plockton

EARLY AUTUMN FROM CREAG NAN GARADH
Plockton and Loch Carron

The Outer Hebrides

LEWIS

Pp.78, 79

Pp.76, 80

Pp.74, 75, 77

P.81

Stornaway

ST. KILDA

Pp.73, 84, 85

NORTH HARRIS

SOUTH HARRIS

Tarbert

P.82

P.83

NORTH UIST

Pp.86, 87

BENBECULA

SOUTH UIST

P.89

BARRA

P.88

VIEW OF BORERAY AND THE STACS

From the Gap, Hirta, St Kilda

Where time stands still

The Outer Hebrides form a long island chain that shelters western Scotland from the full impact of Atlantic storms. In the far south is Berneray which, along with Mingulay, can be reached from Barra, homeland of the Clan Macneil. Ferries serve Barra from Oban.

North of Barra lies South Uist, then Benbecula and North Uist. They are linked by causeways and are renowned for the white sand beaches that line their western coasts, and for the flower-rich machair that lies inland. The Sound of Harris is home to a number of beautiful islands, including a second Berneray. Harris and Lewis actually form one island, Scotland's largest. Lewis has a bleak moorland interior, but a spectacular coastline. Harris is composed of rugged mountains which form a marvellous backdrop to some of the quietest and most beautiful white sand beaches in Europe. Lewis and Harris can be reached by ferry from Ullapool, or from Uig on Skye.

Over forty miles west of North Uist lies Britain's most westerly point, storm-lashed St Kilda, a small group of islands populated until quite recently for perhaps 4000 years by native St Kildans. Their story makes poignant and scarcely believable reading. These great rocks, rising straight out of the vast ocean, are remnants of a huge volcano. Their relative inaccessibility makes them a dream destination for the adventurous traveller.

Setting sun and still water, Tràigh Uuige, Lewis

SALT MARSH AT TRÀIGH NAN SRUBAN
Cradhlastadh, Lewis

76

Nature's patterns echo through time and space, and the shapes formed by sand in an outfall stream literally change in front of our eyes. Nevertheless, these are the very moments of deposition that over aeons give rise to sedimentary rock, such as sandstone. Indeed, two billion years or more later, similar patterns may still be preserved in a metamorphic rock, like gneiss.

My children love the movies, and one of their favourites is *Shrek*, the computer-animated story of a fairy-tale ogre. One choice cameo from the movie has the homeless donkey, voiced by Eddie Murphy, attempting to flatter Shrek; on first seeing the ogre's swampy abode the donkey declares 'I like that boulder, that is a nice boulder.'

Murphy's vocal talent perfectly satirises Shrek's domestic taste, but it is a line that could also have been written for me, for I feel about boulders the way a train spotter must about trains. And Scotland's coast is for the boulder-spotter what Clapham Junction must be for the train-spotter, a little bit of heaven on earth.

Some rocks are made by sediments or tiny organisms gently accumulating in the shallows of river, lake and sea; some are forged in the volcano's furnace; others are cooked and folded by tectonic pressure building the high mountains; yet others are compressed deep under the ocean floor. Whatever their origins, rocks which are exposed become subjected to erosion. Coastal erosion is the ultimate artist of geology. Endless tides and occasional storms ceaselessly and tirelessly undermine cliffs, shift millions of tons of sand, and in the process create rocks and sculpt boulders.

Metamorphic rocks, those changed by heat and pressure, can be found throughout the length of western Scotland. The oldest are found in the Outer Hebrides, including some on South Uist that are nearly three billion years old, making them among the most ancient in the world. This is gneiss (pronounced 'nice', conveniently I feel), of which the form Lewisian gneiss, found chiefly in Lewis and Harris, is the best known. No doubt my children find my enthusiasm for rocks tiresome, but when we were on Lewis they were willing to humour me on those occasions when I could not restrain myself from saying (in an embarrassing impression of Eddie Murphy) 'I like that boulder, that is a gneiss boulder!'

Sand patterns in outfall stream, Tràigh Ghearadha, Lewis

GNEISS BOULDER
Tràigh Uuige, Lewis

78

GNEISS OUTCROP
Cliffs of Dhail Mòr, Lewis

STONES AND SAND
Dhail Mòr beach, Lewis

Mystery still hangs over the apparent astronomical or ritualistic function of the stone circles of Calanais (opposite). Whatever their original purpose, these stones identify this place as sacred, a focal point for humanity in the landscape.

S ited on a low plateau, the great stone circle of Calanais is surrounded on three sides by the sea. This is sheltered seawater, many miles inland from the open ocean. Indeed, when these stones were first raised some five thousand years ago, the sea level was lower, and birch, willow, rowan and hazel grew where the tidal waters of Loch Roag now flow.

There are a number of other Neolithic sites in the area including two stone circles a kilometre to the southeast, but the main circle is much more ambitious and complex than its satellites. The stones remain freely accessible to the general public, which is magical, and remarkable considering the exclusion zone around Stonehenge. On the afternoon of my second visit there a large group of cyclists were amusing themselves among the stones; one of them was riding his mountain bike through the site, noisily proclaiming he was on a pilgrimage. Such behaviour, disrespectful to other visitors and damaging to the site is only likely to ensure that at some point in the future we will no longer be allowed to stand with the stones.

The burial tombs at Maes Howe on Orkney and New Grange in Ireland are contemporary, but in many respects Stonehenge is the only other ancient monument in the British Isles with which the great circle of Calanais can be compared for scale and completeness. Stonehenge may be bigger, but these stones of local Lewisian gneiss, a rock laid down before life on earth had begun, have a presence and power that exceeds their size. From a distance the concentration of stones is striking, but up close their textures and individual personalities are even more so. It is curious to think that the five thousand years for which they have been standing represents a mere one five-hundred-thousandth of the time the rock from which they are made has existed.

Examining the stones in the long summer evening as the sun came and went behind cloud I found myself thinking they were blades of light, bright in shadow, sparkling in sunlight, sharp in profile, fierce in beauty.

Sea stacks, Tràigh Ghearadha, Lewis

80

STANDING STONES
Calanais, Lewis

82

Seilebost, Harris

SHELLS AND SAND
Scarasta, Harris

84

Saint Kilda is the New York City of the seabird world. This squawking cosmopolitan metropolis is a series of fiercely defended ghettoes: gannets, guillemots, black-backed gulls, razorbills, fulmars, puffins, kittiwakes, Manx shearwaters, storm petrels, oyster catchers, snipe, and great skuas, all disputing their territorial boundaries on and around St Kilda's densely populated, skyscraping cliffs.

Conachair, the highest summit, has a near-vertical drop of 1,400 feet (425m) on its northern side, making it the highest sea cliff in the British Isles. Peering over the edge, it extends beyond your peripheral vision, and, like the Grand Canyon, it is impossible to photograph adequately. Far below fulmars practise their avian choreography, but at this distance these birds with their five-foot wingspan are reduced to specks. They look like white midges against the deep sea.

In any other environment the cliffs of Dun would be exceptional. This long narrow island is a single shelf of abruptly sloping grassland on one side, a series of savage cliffs on the other. Steepling peaks and precipices punctuate these cliffs, giving the ridge an appearance of awesome savagery. Yet Dun's highest point is less than half the height of Hirta's cliffs. When a cloud base of 800 feet (240m) shrouds Hirta's main summits of Oiseval, Ruaival and Conachair, Dun can still be in bright sunlight, in a world of its own.

On arrival at Village Bay the visitor receives an ugly reminder of the political imperative of every modern society: defence. South of the St Kilda archipelago and west of Benbecula, a wide expanse of the Atlantic Ocean forms the world's second largest missile range. Range operations are supervised from St Kilda's main island, Hirta, where a base of grey modern buildings, including a small oil-fired power station complete with tanks for over a year's supply of fuel, squat by the beach. On Ruaival and Conachair stand masts, golf ball listening devices, dishes and attendant maintenance buildings.

Soay sheep graze every inch of Hirta accessible to land animals. They are direct genetic descendants of those brought by the early settlers. The National Trust for Scotland has allowed them to graze unmanaged and they have no agricultural function, and no predators (although most are tagged at birth). But by comparison with the ungrazed slopes of Dun the vegetation on Hirta is much poorer and less biologically diverse. I wonder how the Soay sheep will be regarded by future generations, for they seriously undermine biodiversity on St Kilda. Nor do they benefit the long-term preservation of St Kilda's unique archeological remains.

St Kilda is regarded as Europe's greatest seabird colony, and because of this and its archeological remains, UNESCO has recognised its importance by granting it World Heritage Site status. Perhaps one day, if we ever see the folly of firing missiles at each other, the shadow of modern military technology can be lifted and St Kilda's wildness restored.

Geòdha na h-Airdhe, Hirta, St Kilda

85

DUN FROM RUAIVAL
Hirta, St Kilda

In The Scottish Islands *Hamish Haswell-Smith describes the west of Berneray as '... one of the loveliest stretches of white shell sand beach in Britain – about four kilometres of perfection.' If time could stand still, this is one of those places where you believe it would. The sense of space, the visual simplicity of the beach, the colours of the sea, the mountainous backdrop of Harris to the north, and the absolute solitude all combine to defy the twenty-first century. It seemed almost wrong to work in a place so profoundly relaxing. Work usually extracts an emotional toll that can only be repaid with food and sleep, but I felt strangely energised by that afternoon on Berneray. The spell cast on the normally sober and measured Haswell-Smith left its enchantment on me too.*

WILD FLOWERS
Berneray, Sound of Harris

PATH THROUGH DUNES
Berneray, Sound of Harris

Once devastated by the brutality of the Clearances, Barra now offers a sense of great tranquillity. It has been called the Hebrides in miniature and deserves that description, having steep rocky summits such as Heaval, sheltered coves and bays, other islands to north and south, machair, and white sand beaches.

Cockle Strand is one such beach, and uniquely in the British Isles, it also forms the runway for an airport. A greater contrast to the stresses of an international airport is hard to imagine. Your plane or helicopter lands on a vast stretch of firm white sand, onto which you descend. You pick up your luggage and without having to enter any terminal building you are on your way. If you so choose you could cross the road, walk over a field into a dune system and within a few minutes be standing on Tràigh Eais, an utterly deserted beach on the west side of Barra.

For the Outer Hebrides Tràigh Eais is unexceptional – just the same old stretch of breath-taking white sand, the same high dunes on the landward side, the same endlessly fascinating ripples and rivulets, and the same attractive areas of stone that can be found on coasts the length of western Scotland. I wonder, if one lived on Barra, whether this effortless beauty and space would be diminished by familiarity?

The little chain of islands south of Barra includes Mingulay, Pabbay and Berneray, all beautiful and deserted, with little to recommend them except soaring cliffs, huge seabird colonies, ocean skyscapes and on Mingulay the poignant ruins of a village. I shared my boat ride back from there with a dedicated team of sport rock climbers. On those islands you feel you might be the only person for a thousand miles in every direction.

Biulacraig, Mingulay

PASSING CLOUD
Tràigh Eais, Barra

The North West

Cape Wrath

Pp. 91, 94, 102, 103, 110, 111

P.108

Pp.99, 101

P.100

Lochinver

P.96

Pp.92, 97

P.109

P.93

Ullapool

Gairloch

P.98

Pp.95, 106, 107

Pp. 104, 105

WINTER AFTERNOON
Dunes, Balnakiel

Sublime beaches, singular mountains

The north west is regarded by many as the connoisseur's Scotland. This is a remote land, poorly served by public transport, and with no significant centres of population. Few coach tours venture here and, with very few exceptions, caravan sites and gift shops are absent.

Applecross is a place apart. Approaching from the south, it is necessary to cross a high pass, Bealach na Ba. At over 1970 feet (600 m) this is one of Britain's highest, scariest and most spectacular roads. Just to the north the charming village of Shieldaig stands at the gateway of Upper Loch Torridon. Walled in by dark mountains of Torridonian sandstone this extraordinary sea loch is one of Britain's greatest natural wonders. To the north again the coast continues to be deeply incised by bays and lochs. The attractive little beach at Mellon Udrigle is but one of many.

North of Ullapool there is a marked change inland. Mountain ranges give way to loch and lochan-covered moorland, out of which at intervals a single, maverick mountain soars above the surrounding landscape. While not strictly coastal mountains, these great summits form a mesmerising backdrop for beaches such as Achnahaird. Cape Wrath is the northwest corner of the Scottish mainland, but my travels took me just south of here, to Oldshoremore, a beach of quite sublime beauty. East of Cape Wrath is Balnakiel, where a vast dune system stretches out to Faraid Head. Now on the north coast, I also visited Sangobeg, and Loch Eriboll.

Moonlight, Achnahaird

92

LICHENS AND MINERAL STAINING
Mellon Udrigle

94

SUN REFLECTION ON WET SAND
Balnakiel

FROSTED SEAWEED
Ob Mheallaidh, Torridon

96

SUILVEN
From Inverkirkaig

97

STAC POLLAIDH AND CUL BEAG
From Achnahaird

BEALACH NA GAOITHE
Upper Loch Torridon

JUNK-CHOKED OUTFALL STREAM
Oldshoremore

A t the edge of the ocean, nothing holds back the wind. The beaches of Scotland's north-west coast bear the full force of Atlantic weather systems as they swing remorselessly east, usually pirouetting around deep troughs of low pressure. Where the wind blows, sand runs before it, accumulating and drifting in dune systems such as Oldshoremore, and Balnakiel. These are restless landscapes that change as we watch them. Behaving much like snow, dry sand forms ripples and ridges in the wind, though these are softer than the sculpted patterns left by the falling tide.

At Oldshoremore the breeze strengthened to gale force and the sand began to cover my equipment. The crunching of sand between my teeth reminded me of the impact the stuff could have on a lens shutter, a filter or a piece of film. I remembered Death Valley, for working on the dunes there the wind blew so much fine sand into the recesses of my camera bag that I was brushing it off lenses and filters months later. But in Death Valley the heat was oven-like, at Oldshoremore the wind chill and frigid temperatures threatened me with hypothermia.

Although sand may provoke anxieties with equipment it is visually a gift, creating light, colour, and simplification in a landscape composition. While junk and debris can and does gather at the high point of the tide, the intertidal zone of a sandy beach is essentially wiped clean twice a day, giving a powerful sense of space and openness. It is a realm that encourages exercise, refreshment and inspiration, rewarding mind, body and spirit.

At Achmelvich I happened to step out of my camper van around midnight, and saw an aurora borealis overhead in the night sky. It was like a diffuse path of white stardust trailing some celestial Apollo. There are times to be grateful for a call of nature…

100

Hidden cove, Achmelvich

ROCK IN A HARD PLACE
Oldshoremore

102

Army landrovers frequently trundle along the back of Balnakiel beach, on their way to Faraid Head. The Royal Air Force also conducts frequent training flights over this area, a noisy and spectacular reminder that Britain's remotest spots have long been used for military exercises.

TWILIGHT
Balnakiel

SUN SETTING OVER CREAG RIABHACH
Balnakiel Bay

104

WEATHER OVER SKYE'S CUILLIN HILLS
From Applecross

Winter may not be the most obvious time to head down to the sea, especially when temperatures have fallen below freezing. Yet winter produced some of my most memorable experiences of Scotland's coast. A frozen dawn at Upper Loch Torridon provided me with the photographer's ultimate dilemma, too many opportunities. After using the early light for wider landscapes I found a wealth of subject matter in frozen details.

FROZEN MARITIME HEATH
Upper Loch Torridon

WINTER DAWN
Ob Mheallaidh, Upper Loch Torridon

Only tiny settlements appear on the map east of Durness on Scotland's northern shore. There is a beautiful beach at Ceannabeinne, near Sangobeg, which is overlooked by a giant granite erratic. Having explored the shores of Loch Eriboll a little further east I faced the fact that I could not and would not see every beach in Scotland, and headed south once more.

The Summer Isles lie scattered just off the Coigach peninsula north west of Ullapool, and can be reached from the little crofting village of Achiltibuie. From here north to Cape Wrath the mountain ranges that serve as a backdrop to the coast further south are replaced by a series of isolated summits. First come the Inverpolly peaks including Ben More Coigach, Cul Beag, and Stac Pollaidh. Most distinctive of all is Suilven; half neo-classical dome, half Neolithic club, its profile is quite unique. Beyond here are Canisp and the twin-peaked fangs of Quinag, then the bleak stone monoliths of Ben Stack, Arkle, and Foinaven. The names alone are enough to inspire a sense of awe and wonder.

From Achnahaird, many of the southern summits are visible with iconic Stac Pollaidh forming a natural focus. The dunes and beach here are justifiably popular during the summer, when the adjacent field becomes a friendly campsite, with tents and camper vans untidily scattered. Out of season the place returns to a state of Highland loneliness and desolate beauty.

By the standards of the northwest, Lochinver is a heaving metropolis complete with two-way roads, a garage, and even a few shops. From here, and from the nearby hamlet of Inverkirkaig, Suilven can be be glimpsed. With its base hidden by low ridges, and its distance away from you uncertain, it has the presence of an awesome mountain from some unknown, mythic landscape.

Erratic, Sangobeg

CAIRN ON COIGACH
Summer Isles beyond

110

SQUALL TWILIGHT
Balnakiel dunes

WINTER AFTERNOON
Balnakiel Bay

The Northern Isles

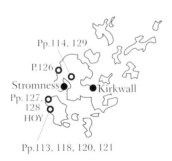

VERTICALLY STRIPED SANDSTONE BOULDERS
Rackwick, Hoy

Far horizons

Ferries serve the Northern Isles from Aberdeen, and from Scrabster and Thurso on Scotland's north coast. The Shetland Isles are Britain's northern outer limit – no land lies between the north coast of Unst and the North Pole. Shetland is closer to Bergen than to Edinburgh and it is perhaps not surprising that culturally the islanders have as much in common with Scandinavians as with their fellow Scots. Shetland is mostly treeless and windswept; heavy glaciation during recent ice ages left many islands and long peninsulas divided by sea lochs, so that nowhere is more than three miles from the coast.

There are also a fantastic abundance of sea stacks and savage rocks offshore.

Much of Orkney is low lying and fertile, but Hoy is a notable exception, being composed of high sandstone moorland and ringed by spectacular cliffs, from which has formed the Old Man of Hoy, Britain's highest sea stack. On Orkney Mainland ancient monuments such as Maes How and the Ring of Brodgar attract the attention of academics as well as the fascination of visitors. Away from these main island groups, Foula and Fair Isle remain inhabited in spite of extreme isolation and challenging weather.

Ring of Brodgar, Orkney Mainland

114

RED CLIFFS AND STACKS
The Neap, Shetland Mainland

116

A calm dry day at Norwick Bay, Unst brought all-encircling cloud which hid the sun and subdued colour. In the soft light drama was missing, but details were revealed and some colours, such as the green of seaweed, positively glowed.

Within the British Isles, a journey to Unst is the closest a traveller can come to a pilgrimage to the end of the world. Land's End and John O'Groats may mark the traditional limits of the United Kingdom, but this is misleading; the Scilly Isles lie to the south and well west of Land's End, while Unst, the northernmost major island in the Shetland archipelago, is 170 miles (275km) north of John O'Groats.

At the northern end of Unst are two headlands, Hermaness and Saxa Vord. Lying just shy of 61° north, they are about 400 miles (640km) south of the Arctic Circle, on the same latitude as Anchorage, Alaska, and Helsinki, Finland's capital. This is even further north than Greenland's Kap Farvel.

On Saxa Vord, jagged rock stacks and an isolated fragment of cliff called the Noup stand at the ocean's edge. Like a shark's fin silhouetted against a setting summer sun, the Noup gave me the main theme I needed in a composition; the miniature offshore island chain form a distant supporting cast. A lighthouse crowns Muckle Flugga, and a little way north of that lies Out Stack. This rock is Britain's northernmost Land's End.

No other habitat on earth magnifies space like the sea. Where the far horizon defines our idea of what is truly flat and truly straight, the sky and ocean fills both our focus and our peripheral vision, and their vastness becomes a metaphor for all possibilities. Ancient seafarers may have feared sailing off the edge of the world, and the brave among them risked doing just that; today we know that however distant the horizon may appear the next land, or perhaps continent, lies a brief plane flight away. But when we contemplate the apparently infinite expanse of ocean from a beach or cliff, in our hearts we can still share the visceral sense of fear, awe and wonder that our forebears felt. In places such as Unst's north coast, when the time and the light is right, many of us experience the greatest sense of space, of freedom, and of adventure we will ever know.

Calm sea, Norwick Bay, Unst

The Noup, Unst

Rackwick is the starting point for the two-mile cliff walk to the Old Man of Hoy. While the Old Man is one fantastic sight for photographers, especially in the late evening light, it is always a wrench to leave Rackwick's unique, compelling boulderscape.

Massive sandstone cliffs rear vertically upwards at either side of Rackwick Bay, which forms the seaward end of a broad glacial valley, overlooked by the biggest hills in the Northern Isles. Glacial moraines, vast piles of heather-covered rubble deposited by retreating glaciers, are clearly evident, including one that overlooks the beach itself.

Light sands create an idyllic beach on the eastern side, but sandstone boulders fill the larger, western part of the bay. These were formed from the cliffs, whose regular geometric faulting fractures into approximately cuboid blocks. Thus, the cliffs are a geological proto-boulder factory. The sea does the finishing work over the centuries; regular tidal washes punctuated by gales and storms grind and tumble away the hard edges. The result can only be described as Boulder Central, a remarkable wealth of spheroid and ovoid stones that surpasses the imagination.

The sandstone from which these boulders are made has well-defined bedding planes and contains many minerals in varying concentrations, so they are infinitely varied and colourful. Further out in the intertidal zone, weed and marine lichens have colonised the boulders, turning them green or brown. But towards the top of the tide, where the sea's influence diminishes, the colour of the sandstone is dispayed in a painterly riot of hoops, planes, extrusions and contours. Some spherical examples have rings reminiscent of Saturn's. If there is a more spectacular example of nature's art anywhere in the British Isles I have yet to see it.

Low tide, Rackwick, Hoy

BETTER THAN PASTA
Seaweed, Hillswick, Shetland

SOFT LIGHT DAWN
Rackwick, Hoy

TIDAL FLOW
Rackwick, Hoy

122

VILLIANS OF URE
Esha Ness, Shetland

TWILIGHT
St Ninian's Isle, Shetland

BEACH PEBBLES
Fladdabister, Shetland

126

As a young photographer I met Chris Bonington (who I photographed for a Country Life article) about twenty-five years after I first saw him on TV climbing the Old Man of Hoy. Another fourteen years later I went to Hoy myself. Bonington has always been one of my heroes, but I hope he can understand if I say that I found the Old Man of Hoy more exciting to photograph.

Shetland must have a higher concentration of sea stacks than anywhere else in Scotland. These great towers of rock, each one unique, symbolise the wild world. Essentially untameable, their only 'function' is to house nesting seabirds. They are the last remaining true wilderness in Britain.

In spite of the abundance of stacks off Shetland, though, it is Orkney that boasts the greatest stack of all. This is the Old Man of Hoy, a pillar of sandstone that towers 450 feet (137m) above the sea. It sits on harder basalt, which serves as a pedestal, with its top around the high tide mark. Like all stacks the Old Man is a fragment of cliff that has been isolated from its parent by erosion.

One of the first pieces of TV I remember seeing was the original ascent of the Old Man by Chris Bonington, Tom Patey and Rusty Bailie in 1966. The climb looked sensational enough, but what stuck in my eight-year-old mind was the climbers enduring assault from spitting fulmars defending their territory. Modern equipment and techniques may have rendered the Old Man a slightly less formidable climb than it once was, but it is still an awesome sight. No one could call it beautiful, however. Its layered structure suggests a colossal stack of giant pancakes, but a stack that has been savagely hacked about by a bad-tempered chef. One day the sea will cause it to fall, but it is impossible to say when.

The cliffs to the north reach up to St John's Head, which at 1,150 feet (350 m) dwarfs the Old Man. This is a challenging landscape to hike around with 20kg of camera gear. To explore different angles on the Old Man requires close investigation of the clifftops, where one false step on a vertical drop would mean certain death. Giant skuas patrol their nesting territory on the moorland behind, and dive bomb unsuspecting photographers with no provocation. A tripod held above my head proved a handy deterrent.

Yesnaby Castles, Orkney

THE OLD MAN OF HOY

128

The Old Man of Hoy

FIRST LIGHT
Ring of Brodgar

The East

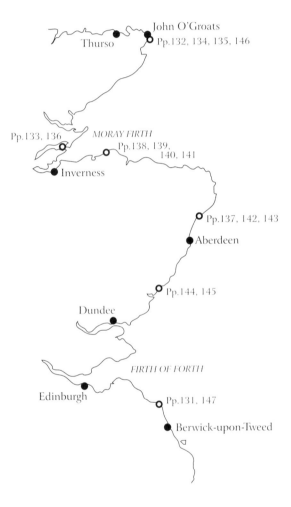

John O'Groats
Thurso

MORAY FIRTH
Inverness

Aberdeen

Dundee

FIRTH OF FORTH
Edinburgh
Berwick-upon-Tweed

SEABIRD COLONIES
Cliffs at St Abb's Head

Stacks, sand dunes and seabirds

The east coast of Scotland is much less convoluted than the west, and indeed seems almost to belong to a different country. Scotland's mountain ranges are rarely visible from the coast, but they provide shelter from the prevailing westerly winds and thus endow the east with a far more favourable climate. There are no islands offshore, with the exceptions of the Isle of May, and the Bass Rock in the Firth of Forth.

The great stacks of Duncansby Head make a spectacular focal point in the far north east. Scotland's oil industry dominates Cromarty Firth, where a small fleet of giant oil drilling rigs looms offshore. A number of pleasant seaside towns lie on the Moray coast, where the wonders of weathered sandstone can be seen at Cove Bay. North of Aberdeen, Forvie is a great dune system with National Nature Reserve status. St Cyrus is another National Nature Reserve, where wild salmon are still caught in fixed nets. Golf courses and pretty fishing villages line the Fife coast between the Firths of Tay and Forth. In the south, St Abb's Head near the English border is one of Britain's most important seabird breeding sites.

Sea Stacks, Duncansby Head

SAND PATTERNS AND OIL RIGS
Cromarty Firth

The most striking feature of this north-eastern outpost of Scotland's mainland are two great sea stacks. In the half light before dawn these are dragon's fangs, primeval, monumental, otherworldly. To the north, the cliffs are split by deep ravines known as geos; these are an early stage in the process of erosion which creates the stacks. Vertical weaknesses in the sedimentary rock are exposed and amplified by wave action. Although complicated by sea level changes, earth movements and ice ages it is not hard to see how what are now headlands created by geos will become isolated and, eventually, separated from the mainland to create further sea stacks. Although this process is unimaginably slow on a human scale, it is nevertheless utterly remorseless and inevitable.

This natural grandeur stands in sharp contrast to the tourist trap of John O'Groats just a mile or so to the west. Barely more than a hamlet, this tiny settlement has exploited its status as mainland Scotland's most northerly point (although, as any map will show, this distinction actually belongs to Dunnet Head, further west) to attract visitors by the jumbo jet load. The unfortunate consequence is a cluster of souvenir shops and cafes whose sole purpose is to part people from their holiday money. On the other hand, since I used the facilities, had a coffee and bought a map here, perhaps I shouldn't be too critical.

Back at Duncansby Head, a car park, a lighthouse and the neatly divided fields inland are reminders that this is no wild landscape. But the eternal cycles and energy of the wild world, symbolised by the stacks and clearly evident in the roaring waters of the Pentland Firth to the north, still reign just offshore. Compared to our materialistic, excessively busy, and ultimately rather short lives these inscrutable and apparently never-ending forces of nature may provide some perspective.

Dawn comes early to northern Scotland in mid-June. At 4 a.m. the sun's rim appeared north of north east on the horizon. As I set up my camera equipment haunting cries, somewhere between a song and a howl came from far below. Whales perhaps? Or some bird I didn't recognise? A little later, on descending to the beach, I discovered the source of the noise. Scores of seals hauled out on the rocks at low tide were squabbling and jostling for the best accommodation.

Sea stacks, summer sunrise, Duncansby Head

FORESHORE AND FINE WEATHER
Duncansby Head

The oil rigs of Cromarty Firth are out of commission, and essentially in storage. In spite of my environmentalist instincts I found them strangely compelling, and on the occasions when my route took me this way I would invariably stop and attempt a photograph.

Arriving in my camper van late at night on the shores of Nigg Bay, I felt overwhelmed by the industrial character of the place. Vast installations on land and the drilling rigs of Cromarty Firth offshore, their lights blazing, filled the senses.

The following morning I set off before dawn expecting that I might make a picture to illustrate the melancholy fate of a landscape subjugated by the oil industry. Eventually I found a point above Balnapaling where I could take in fourteen drilling platforms in a single sweep of the eye, and nine could be included in one composition made with my longest lens. These platforms must be some of the largest mobile structures ever made, and would tower over most ships. It is hard not to be impressed by their scale, and some even have a certain functional elegance. On the shore below I found thriving mussel colonies, and richly-sculpted sand ripples. The top of the beach was, if anything, surprisingly free from polluting flotsam and jetsam, and a dune system seemed to be healthy. Inland, snow banks still decorated distant mountains, and only the lightest breeze disturbed the clean, clear air. Somehow it was all so much pleasanter than I had expected. The rigs were really good subject matter for photography and, in spite of what they represent, the sharp end of humanity's almost desperate dependence on fossil fuels, with all that implies, the coastal environment seemed relatively intact.

Cromarty Firth might be a place most people in search of nature would avoid, yet as a landscape with a human story to tell it is one of the most interesting I have seen. It was a useful reminder to me that nature and industry can co-exist.

Oil rigs, Balnapaling, Cromarty Firth

TANGLED ROPE, PRE-DAWN
Forvie National Nature Reserve

138

The best bit of Cove Bay is reached through a
natural tunnel in the rock, and on my second visit
I spent a happy three and a half hours here at low
tide, exploring the cliffs, caves, and rock pools. But
the most visually enchanting aspect of the beach
was the pebbles and the way they were
accommodated by the sandstone rock platform
beneath. There were so many possible images to be
taken that I had to ration myself to a few
photographs, and resolve to return in the future.

SANDSTONE CAVE

Cove Bay

PEBBLES ON SANDSTONE PAVEMENT
Cove Bay

PEBBLES
Cove Bay

EVENING LIGHT
Moray Firth, from Hopeman shore

142

The extensive sandy beach, the high dunes, the bird life, the sense of space and the solitude make Forvie NNR a truly special place. Throughout the day I spent there I saw fewer than half a dozen other souls.

DUNES

Forvie National Nature Reserve

FOUR VIEWS, ONE MORNING
Sands of Forvie

144

SALMON NET
St Cyrus National Nature Reserve

145

St Cyrus National Nature Reserve

Anyone who found Hitchcock's classic film, The Birds, unwatchably scary, may well prefer to avoid St Abb's Head. It is one of Scotland's most important seabird colonies and during the nesting season the cliffs are so alive with the sound and motion of kittiwakes, guillemots, and razorbills, not to mention the aroma of guano, that anyone half-hearted about this feathered fraternity will feel intimidated.

Hitchcock also directed Vertigo, another sensation that can be experienced at St Abbs. But the awesome cliffs and stacks just offshore can be exhilarating. I felt compelled to get as close as I could to the edge of the cliffs and peer over the precipice.

YELLOW LICHENS
Duncansby Head

FOLDED CLIFFS
St Abb's Head

Coast of wonder

Something about the coast has always lifted my spirit. Mountains too, where land seems to reach for the heavens, have inspired me from childhood and still do. Scotland is a nation of sea and mountains, so it is no exaggeration to say that, as an assignment, this book was a dream come true.

But what makes the coast, particularly Scotland's, so special? Someone who already loves wild coastline might be surprised that I should even pose the question. Yet I would like to know: why does it inspire us so, this coast of Scotland with its dark moods, difficult journeys, and infuriatingly unpredictable weather? Is there a simple explanation? Perhaps, but trying to analyse its attractions from a detached perspective is all but impossible.

Two hundred, or five hundred, or one thousand years ago, native Scots or their rare visitors would surely have seen it rather differently. Though we do not know for sure, we can perhaps guess how their needs, motivations, and cultural environment might have governed their attitude. The sea itself might have meant trade and wealth to some, fish to others, and for yet others escape, and freedom from persecution. But it would also have brought danger and fear in the form of storms, floods, and during the Dark Ages, Scandinavian raiders.

In contrast, our perspective is privileged. Protected by the peace, prosperity and technology of the twenty-first century, most of us do not need to ask how this frontier between land and sea can sustain us, shelter us or provide for us. It seems to exist almost purely for our recreational enjoyment. We see somewhere to fish perhaps, but only

for sport. Golfers will appreciate the wonderful links courses. Some seek out cliffs for climbing, others look for opportunities to paddle a canoe, or sail, or swim. The creatively inclined may be inspired to paint a water-colour, or photograph a sunset; still others come to walk, to play, or just to sit and think.

While some local people do still make a living from this environment, farming, fishing, fish farming, and in some areas drilling for oil, the rest of us value its timeless beauty, and its wildness. To visitors, scenic quality is perhaps this coast's single greatest asset. Does the view of non-residents matter though? Well, those of us who visit, whether Scots, fellow-Britons, or travellers from beyond our islands, are increasingly vital to the local economy. So our thoughts and feelings do count. Those who say 'You can't eat scenery' must come to terms with an age that increasingly values and cherishes our remaining natural landscapes. With luck economics will show that sustaining the coast's physical beauty and biodiversity does pay in the long term.

In the quest for explanations, I think it is impossible to provide a single unifying theory of what makes coast, and especially Scotland's coast, quite so magical and uplifting. If there is one thing that strikes me in retrospect as I reflect on my journeys, it is the extraordinary variety of landscapes on offer. Some places seemed largely about space. Others offered a wealth of textures and colour. Some were steeped in human history that still lingers in the rocks. Energy and detail impressed me on some beaches, while the monumental scale of awesome cliffs took my breath away elsewhere. What all had in common

148

was the slow rhythm of the tides, and of the seasons. And just when I had decided that the symbols of wildness provided the collective thread of inspiration, a lonely lighthouse or abandoned croft would remind me that we humans are an intrinsic part of this landscape, and our presence can be enhancing. Wherever I went I found differing aspects to focus on, and with the exception of the weather, almost nothing disappointed me.

But, paradoxically, it is precisely because of the weather that Scotland retains its unbreakable connection to the wild world. The beaches of South Harris are among the most beautiful in Europe, but if they enjoyed a Mediterranean climate then perhaps by now they would have a backdrop of high-rise hotels, instead of rocky mountains. The same dire prospect would face any number of beaches in the north west, and on the Islands. The weather, and to a lesser degree the midges, help protect the allure of these landscapes. Those of us who visit must risk the likelihood of wind, cloud, rain and midge bites most of the time; but when the rain stops, the clouds part, the wind drops, and the midges are not biting, we can revel in sights so sublime that we will forgive Scotland everything. And only those who can tolerate weather will ever see them.

Even in summer I rarely walked without a fleece top, for the sea's damp breezes cool the warmest summer day. On cold but spectacular winter mornings, when ice could be found fringing the inshore waters, I felt especially fortunate. I remained warm in modern outdoor gear, and felt a heightened sense of creative challenge in the sharp air and low sunlight. Is it work in such conditions? How lucky can you be?

Landscape photographers have always favoured sunrise and sunset, even before the days of colour photography. This does not necessarily mean pointing the camera at some vivid sky and forgetting everything else.

Rather it means attempting to record faithfully the infinitely subtle colours of early and late light, when warm and cold tones contrast beautifully, and when the light creates a mood both beguiling and mysterious. With its epic skyscapes and rapidly changing weather conditions, the best sunrises and sunsets of Scotland's coast would have my vote for the Greatest Show on Earth.

When conditions were unhelpful I had more time to just walk, to look, to think, and to wonder. On rocky shores and clifftops, my attention was devoted to keeping my footing and avoiding injury. This encourages an eye for detail. But on long, sandy beaches, a dead flat surface and a great sense of space inspires the brain itself to coast, allowing free association of thought, observations, memories and ideas. When the sun was too high and bright, or the cloud blanket too uniform, I enjoyed what were (perhaps ironically) my most creative moments. Freed from the need to photograph I found the rhythms of walking and the absence of material distractions a mind-expanding combination that encouraged rumination on the vastness of time, the nature of light and the astonishing beauty of a tiny shell.

My journeys to the outer limits of Scotland's coast and its islands have left me with a kaleidoscopic cascade of memories that flow through my thoughts and dreams, and leave me yearning to return. Although human settlements can be found everywhere, nature's beauty and majesty remain alive here, and overall it is this sense of a land still little changed by human activity that make it so powerfully appealing for the adventurous traveller.

I still imagine Iona, visualise Oldshoremore, muse on Mull, and reflect on Rackwick, where water, and light, and rock and living things are still free; in these places my soul still wanders. Scotland's shores draw my imagination, fill my dreamtime, lift my spirits. In my heart I hold Scotland's coast, a coast of wonder.

Reflections

Almost all the photographs in this book were made with an Ebony 45SU. This is a hand-made 5x4 inch non-folding wooden field camera with interchangeable bellows. The main lens used was a Rodenstock Grandagon-N 90mm f/4.5, but I also used a Nikkor-W 150mm f/5.6, a Schneider Super-Angulon XL 72mm f/5.6, a Rodenstock Sironar 180mm f/5.6, a Nikkor-W 210mm f/5.6, a Fujinon-T 300mm f/8, a Nikkor-T 360mm f/8 and a Nikkor-T 500mm f/11. A Mamiya 7 rangefinder camera was also used on Eigg.

Throughout I used professional Fujichrome film, both Velvia 50 and Velvia 100F. My Lee system filters helped me achieve colour and exposure balance in-camera. All my light metering was done manually with a Pentax digital spotmeter.

Various tripods were used, depending on the circumstances. These included a Manfrotto 055, a Gitzo carbon fibre Mountaineer, and a Benbo 1. They were equipped with a Manfrotto 405 or 410 head. The equipment was carried in a Lowepro Pro-Trekker backpack.

I get asked all the time whether I am 'shooting on digital yet?' as if it is inevitable, sooner or later. I do not see it that way. So long as I get the results I want with film there seems no reason to change. I believe the future of photography will be a creative, peaceful co-existence between film and digital.

My field notes below are not a comprehensive analysis of every picture in the book, but rather a brief reflection, or thought, on those I consider most important. I hope they offer some insight.

150

P. 11 Low tide, Machrie Bay, Arran
Strong low sunlight skimming across rippled lines of sand helps convey depth and texture. But here the blue sky overhead meant little reflected light, resulting in dark shadows, and the black seaweed lacks detail. The image is perhaps a little too dependent on its strong perspective.

P. 16 Rockpool in sandstone, Corrie, Arran
Sandstone makes a magical coastal rock, since its layered structure readily assumes wonderfully sculpted shapes under weathering. Isolating the pool from its wider environment helps emphasise its curving form.

P. 13 High cliffs, Mull of Galloway
Bright sun but hazy light provided good illumination for the colourful wild flowers and lichen on the steep cliffs, without evoking much in the way of atmosphere. I tried to restore some drama by shooting from extremely close to the cliff's edge.

P. 17 Arran from Ardneil Bay
The brilliant greens of seaweed enliven the dark tones of a rock platform, while in the distance the sun has already dropped behind Arran. The tilt mechanism of a view camera allows sharp focus throughout the picture space.

P. 15 Soft sunset, Culzean Bay
Having the sun in the picture is a risky tactic, but it can be done in soft hazy light as the sun's disc approaches the horizon. A complex sandstone foreshore and gold reflections in the sea helped compensate for a relatively featureless sky.

P. 19 Granite erratics, Corrie, Arran
A large area of cloud in the east kept blocking the sun, so this dawn picture was harder to make than it looks. Erratic boulders are the main subject, but the composition also relies on perspective from the rock platform, and the punctuation of Holy Island's summit in the far distance.

P.20 Squill, Mull of Galloway
Partly shady light helps preserve the naturally blue colour of squill, which flourishes on these cliffs. A normal lens frames a simple, unspectacular scene where detail predominates.

P.30 Three shells, Loch na Mile, Jura
To begin with, this dark grey sand seemed an impossible subject. But it is this very darkness that helps emphasise the tones and shapes of the shells. A strong linear perspective suggests depth.

P.21 Lichen-covered rocks, Drumadoon, Arran
Just as the sun was setting I spotted these fangs of rock, and managed to make one exposure before the light died. It was about as close as I ever get to making a 'grab shot', and fortunately the camera was already fitted with the right lens.

P.31 Tidal inlet, Machir Bay, Islay
I climbed high to search for an elevated viewpoint from the south of Machir Bay. But in the end I found myself back near sea level, where the textures and shapes of the rock better evoked the smell and sensations of the seashore.

P.23 Windy day, Machrie Bay, Arran
As the caption suggests the wind was strong, obliging me to adopt a low angle in the hope of keeping the camera as steady as possible. The cloudscape changed endlessly, and every so often a little sunlight in the distance helped lift the atmosphere.

P.32 Cattle grazing on dunes, Loch Gruinart, Islay
As well as geese, for which it is famous, Loch Gruinart is home to many free-ranging cattle that graze its northwestern shores. The stately pace of their grazing rhythm allows even the large format photographer to capture the action!

151

P.25 Winter afternoon, Luing
Intense colour characterises a sunlit winter afternoon, making this a special time of year for photography. A long lens was used here to draw in the distant village of Cullipool, and a small aperture with a long exposure assured enough depth of focus.

P.33 Dune, Machir Bay, Islay
In the warm light of a setting sun the dunes that back the great sandy beach of Machir Bay turn a dull gold. A simple composition emphasises colour and atmosphere rather than detail.

P.27 Decaying hull, Luing
My instinct here was to use a long lens to make an abstract close-up image, and emphasise the textures. But try as I might something was always distracting. On the verge of giving up I had a quick look with a wide lens and everything fell into place.

P.34 Stone jetty, Keilmore, Paps of Jura beyond
An air temperature of –6°C greeted me on this morning as well as a magical pre-dawn glow, and almost perfectly still air. From this stone jetty the Paps of Jura were just visible, but within minutes of this picture being taken they disappeared beneath the burgeoning cloud.

P.29 Quiet dawn, Craighouse harbour
I searched the coast here for an hour before dawn, but I searched in vain if I sought the sun. Instead, soft light and reflections gave me something subtler than I had expected. The sky thinned and brightened briefly, and that was the moment I made this picture.

P.35 Sea loch shallows, midwinter, Loch na Cille
In theory, sea ice can only develop below –7°C, due to the salt content. In practice, fresh water run-off reduces salinity in sheltered inshore waters, and I found icy sheets on sea water several times during my winter forays.

P.37 Thrift growing in granite, Fidden, Mull
Sea pink, or thrift, has an uncanny ability to cling to the most improbable niches of a coastal habitat. Its presence here was the perfect excuse for a close up on the textures and colours of Mull's pink granite.

P.39 Weather over Burg and the Sound of Mull, from Kintra
Wide-angle views over coastal landscapes may seem routine, but every one seems to throw up its own challenges. Timing was crucial here; the weather system in the background mattered, but so did catching the all-too-brief moment of sun on the foreground rocks.

P.40 Granite foreshore, Fidden, Mull
Behind this viewpoint is one of the best located campsites in Scotland. While I made photographs during a beautiful sunset my companions cooked an excellent pasta meal with a vegetarian sauce. That is my strongest memory associated with this picture!

P.41 Thrift and granite islands, Fidden, Mull
Fidden overlooks the southern end of the Sound of Iona, and it was from here that my companions and I began our kayaking trip around that famous island. But Fidden's superb granite shoreline and sandy beach make it a photographic destination in its own right.

P.43 Hexagonal basalt detail, vault of Fingal's Cave, Staffa
Looking at the cold, precise geometry of Fingal's Cave vault, it is hard to believe this rock was once boiling hot, molten lava. The attraction of this example was the mildew staining around the cracks, which, for me, creates an image within an image.

P.45 Fingal's Cave, Staffa
On first glance, Fingal's Cave seemed as black as a coalmine. As my eyes adjusted to the darkness, amazing detail emerged from the gloom, but exposing it correctly and evenly in this wide-angle view still proved quite a challenge.

152

P.46 Tideline at twilight, Iona
The intense pink glow following sunset is hard to convey on film, and I wanted to make a picture that caught the mystery of that light. A long exposure of this fragment of shoreline is unable to render detail in the water, rendering instead insubstantial traces of its flow over the sand and shingle.

P.47 White Strand of the Monks, Iona
The massacre of innocent monks on this beach by Viking raiders makes grim reading, but today it is hard to imagine a more peaceful place in the world. The last sunlight skims sand and dune grass, its pink rays balancing the blue of the sky.

P.48 Sanna Bay and the Small Isles, Ardnamurchan
Shot on a windy winter afternoon, it was hard to keep the camera steady. But spectacular, changeable light inspired me to keep trying!

P.49 Dune grasses, Ardnamurchan
I spotted these grasses only minutes before the sun was destined to sink below a distant headland. It is usually said that large format photographers must anticipate rather than react to the moment, but in this case I managed to break the rules.

P.50 Inland sea, Pap of Glen Coe from Kinlochleven
Sea lochs that penetrate deep into the Scottish interior, such as Loch Leven, are naturally far more sheltered than seawater exposed to the restless motion of the Atlantic. I set out to show the stillness and, consequently, the reflections that result.

P.51 Three horsemen (no Apocalypse), Castle Stalker, Loch Linnhe
Roads, quarries, towns and bridges line the shores of the Firth of Lorn, but at least Castle Stalker makes a picturesque contribution to this landscape. When three horseriders appeared, I knew timing would be critical. I set my camera to freeze their movement and made just one exposure.

P.53 Bay of Laig, Eigg
As soon as I saw Rùm's mountainous profile I was hooked. Finding fascinating foreground material to complement this great backdrop at the Bay of Laig was not difficult, although keeping the theme simple and clear sometimes was.

P.55 Calm evening, Morar
When faced with a gift of pure light I have often been guilty of overcomplicating things. Here, faced with almost nothing but sea and a glorious, fast-fading sunset, and with one sheet of film left in my camera bag, I found the confidence to keep things simple.

P.57 Late afternoon, Rùm from Bay of Laig, Eigg
Such light in such a place is no everyday event, and I found myself thinking my whole life had led to this moment; for a landscape photographer it was a moment of total focus.

P.58 Sandstone slot canyon, Camas Sgiotaig, Eigg
This defile in the sandstone, carved by a stream, reminded me of slot canyons I know in Arizona, hence the caption. Lit only by the blue sky overhead I knew a strong blue cast was inevitable, and deliberately left it unfiltered.

P.59 Frost on seaweed, Loch Duich
The sun may not reach this shoreline at all through the winter months, and this frost was photographed late one afternoon. Anchored to the tiny stone, the seaweed seems to burst through the top of the frame, emphasising its life force (so I like to think!).

P.60 Late sunlight, mouth of River Morar
The deep shadows in these rocks illustrate how very difficult it can sometimes be to create good landscape photographs. To the eye the strong sunlight looked wonderful, but the resulting contrast almost exceeded the range of the film.

P.61 Winter afternoon, Five Sisters of Kintail from Loch Duich
Blue skies overhead mean blue light in the shadows. In this landscape warm sunlight on the snowy mountains helped balance the colour, but it was nearly impossible to balance the brightness of the snow with the darkness of the shoreline.

P.63 Cuillin from Elgol, Skye
It is only very rarely I would choose to photograph an open landscape in such grey light as this. However, this is how Scotland often looks, and to me at least it is still beautiful. Making images in 'poor' light is a real creative challenge.

P.64 Sunlit stones, Bay of Laig, Eigg
Stones and rocks may be inanimate, but their sculptural power still gives them life. When I find a place with strong geology I feel I am surrounded by living things and try to use light and composition to suggest just that.

P.65 Incoming tide, Elgol, Skye
When weathered, many rocks have a fluid energy that suggests the movement of water. This picture was taken just as the tide moved over the top part of the picture, which I think emphasises that quality.

P.66 Summer evening, Neist Point, Skye
High above the sea and totally exposed to the prevailing westerly winds, the challenge here was to keep the camera still. The photograph was made as a rare shaft of sunlight passed over the headland. Cloud over the distant cliffs (far left) illustrate the unsettled nature of the weather.

P.67 Isolated basalt pillar, Mointeach nan Tarbh, Skye
I discovered this remarkable feature as it was getting dark, some distance from my car. I decided to make a photograph anyway, and was glad I did for the dim blue light conveys a sense of mystery that suits the subject.

P. 68 Summer dawn, Old Man of Storr, Trotternish, Skye
In June a very early start is required to reach this viewpoint in time for dawn. A tough uphill hike precedes any photographic activities, for only an elevated view really works here, and the walk begins nearly a thousand feet below the towers.

P. 69 Soft light, hard rock, Elgol, Skye
This round boulder has special memories for me. It was the focus of an image used on the cover of my book First Light. This picture was made in much less spectacular conditions, but the low contrast of soft light reveals subtle detail and colour.

P. 70 After rain, summer morning, Plockton
The picturesque elements of this scene proved irresistible, though I worried the content might seem clichéd. A very bright sky made balancing exposure almost impossible, but the soaking foreground prompted me to make the picture anyway.

154

P. 71 Early autumn on Creag nan Gáradh, Plockton and Loch Carron
Plockton's superb setting made it the Scottish coastal village I most wanted to photograph. This hillside, owned by The National Trust for Scotland, proved a good vantage point and a great source of early autumn colour.

P. 73 View of Boreray and the stacs, from the Gap, Hirta, St Kilda
My visit to St Kilda was poor for weather, and I was obliged to take what opportunities I could whenever the sun appeared. Clouds trailing from the summit of Boreray show how these isolated rocks are big enough to create their own weather systems.

P. 75 Salt marsh at Tràigh nan Sròban, Cradhlastadh, Lewis
As soon as I saw it I knew I wanted to use the serpentine shape of this stream to lead the eye through the salt marsh to the bay and mountains beyond. Very little light reflected from the water's surface in the foreground however, creating quite a dark mood, in spite of the sunlight.

P. 77 Gneiss boulder, Tràigh Uuige, Lewis
The shape of this boulder was hardly beautiful, but the colours of the rock were so strong it just cried out to be photographed. Soft light helped reveal detail and control contrast.

P. 78 Gneiss outcrop, cliffs of Dhail Mòr, Lewis
I arrived a little late at this point to capture the light I'd hoped for, but there was just enough pink in the remnants of light to lift the foreground rock. A superwide lens helped show context and strengthen perspective.

P. 79 Stones and sand, Dhail Mòr beach, Lewis
The beaches of Lewis do inspire a minimalist approach, for the sand and stones are so beautiful that they deserve study without elaboration. A lot of care is required when scouting to avoid treading on sand that may eventually feature in a composition.

P. 81 Standing stones, Calanais, Lewis
I had seen many images of these great stones before my visit, but none showing that this is a coastal location. The sea is only three hundred yards away, but the position of the stones meant that, short of scaffolding, I could only show a small strip of seawater in the background.

P. 82 Sun setting over Taransay, Seilebost, Harris
This had been a clear day, but it was remarkable how the clouds developed and the light softened. This proved ideal light to shoot into, as the sun's rays scattered and weakened behind veils of moisture and atmosphere.

P. 83 Shells and sand, Scarasta, Harris
I had hoped to photograph these shells in skimming sunlight but by the time I had found my spot the sun had disappeared. By opting for a wide lens and a very low viewpoint I was able to restore a little of the drama now missing from the light.

P.85 Dun from Ruaival, Hirta, St Kilda
The composition I wanted for this picture could only be accomplished with my widest lens, and the steep downward perspective helped emphasise Dun's savage cliffs. Poor weather may even have helped emphasise mood and atmosphere.

P.86 Wild flowers, Berneray, Sound of Harris
Soft light encouraged me to attempt an extreme piece of close focussing here, which I would have avoided in sunlight. Very light winds allowed me to work low to the beach without fear of sand blowing all over my camera gear.

P.87 Path through dunes, Berneray, Sound of Harris
This is a simple composition that depends on the visual journey suggested by the path as well as the sheer unspoilt beauty of the scene. Soft light creates a world of subtle, delicate colours.

P.89 Passing cloud, Tràigh Eais, Barra
The sun had already disappeared earlier on this afternoon, but just when I thought the moment had passed this intriguing cloud started forming over the sea. As it moved inland it briefly seemed to echo the forms on the beach, creating something from almost nothing.

P.91 Winter afternoon, dunes, Balnakiel
Something about the loneliness and intense colour of winter by the sea makes it very special. Balnakiel is one of the remotest beaches in Scotland too, and the light on this afternoon truly did it justice.

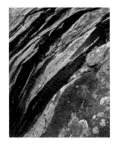

P.93 Lichens and mineral staining, Mellon Udrigle
The beach at wonderfully named Mellon Udrigle is pretty, with tremendous views to An Teallach in the east. But this steep bank of rock with its vivid colours distracted me. Compound view camera movements allowed me to achieve sharp detail throughout.

P.94 Sun reflection on wet sand, Balnakiel
As a student I made a black and white photograph on an Anglesey beach of the sun's reflection in wet sand, which I still consider one of my best images. This is as close as I have come to recreating it in colour.

P.95 Frosted seaweed, Ob Mheallaidh, Torridon
Personally I associate the seaside with mild or warm weather, so the sight of frost transforming the familiar elements of the coastal environment had great novelty value for me. However, novelty alone is not a good reason to make a picture; I still had to make a visually convincing, technically correct study.

P.96 Suilven from Inverkirkaig
I hunted for this image on numerous occasions, and on none was I fortunate with the light. When the autumn was at its height I felt that, even in the soft light, there was enough colour and detail to carry the composition.

P.97 Stac Pollaidh and Cul Beag from Achnahaird
I used a longer lens than normal to bring the distant summits nearer to the foreground. The image is unfiltered for colour to preserve the strong blue light on the mountains.

P.98 Bealach na gaoithe, Upper Loch Torridon
Above the village of Inveralligin is an area of scattered glacial erratics, composed of Torridonian sandstone. The subtle reds and russets of autumn helped balance the cold light of a cloudy afternoon.

P.99 Junk-choked outfall stream, Oldshoremore
I was motivated by both sadness and anger in making this photograph, for Oldshoremore is one of Scotland's most wild and beautiful beaches. Yet I still wanted to create a compositon that evoked depth, and a sense of place.

P. 101 Rock in a hard place, Oldshoremore
Uncannily wedged, this giant boulder seemed a
compelling subject, but with the great drawback of
being in the shade while its background of sand was
brightly sunlit. However, much high cloud gave
sufficient fill-in light to allow me good exposure with
careful balancing filtration.

P. 102 Twilight, Balnakiel
Rain was already falling by the time I opened
the shutter, and after the twenty-two second
exposure was finished I decided to preserve my
camera from a soaking by packing down.
Fortunately, I had what I wanted, one of the
advantages of trying to make every shot count.

P. 103 Sun setting over Creag Riabhach,
Balnakiel Bay
Sometimes a very simple composition is all
that's needed to show the essence of light and
space that make a beach like Balnakiel so
special.

P. 104 Jellyfish, Applecross
I have seen beached jellyfish before, but never in the
abundance I discovered here near Applecross village. I
used a standard lens, and made the dark red jellyfish
become the focus around which the composition revolves.

P. 105 Weather over Skye's Cuillin Hills,
from Applecross
Caught between the line of jellyfish on the high tide
mark and the spectacular mountainous backdrop, I
attempted to resolve the issue with a foreground to
background design. Fast-changing conditions gave
moments of strong backlighting on the jellyfish.

P. 106 Frozen maritime heath,
Upper Loch Torridon
I was struck by the idea that this frozen pool was
a blue contour map. It was extremely tricky to
manoeuvre around it without disturbing the ice or
frosted grasses, but when I had finally positioned
the tripod everything seemed to fit.

P. 107 Winter dawn, Ob Mheallaidh, Upper
Loch Torridon
When the air temperature is –3°C, and the sun
appears early to gild the mountains of one of
Scotland's most spectacular landscapes, that is a
dawn to remember! All I had to do was keep my
wits about me.

P. 109 Cairn on Coigach, Summer Isles beyond
The Summer Isles have always had a magical
appeal for me, partly because of their name, and
partly for their remoteness. I wanted to
photograph them on a summer sunset, but sadly
never had the conditions for it. This bright
summer day was the best I could do.

P. 110 Squall, twilight, Balnakiel dunes
The high dunes on the way to Faraid Head are a
wonderful vantage point over the remote northern
coast of Scotland. With the sun already gone
down and the light fading fast I kept the shutter
open for two minutes to make this picture.

P. 111 Winter afternoon, Balnakiel Bay
This wide-angle composition looks simple enough,
but in reality I struggled to get all the elements
successfully resolved before the sun disappeared
behind land to the west.

P. 113 Vertically striped sandstone boulders,
Rackwick, Hoy
In many locations the main problem is finding
something that works. Here it was one of deciding
what to select from an embarrassment of riches. I
chose the foreground stone because of its remarkable
range of colours.

P. 115 Red cliffs and stacks, the Neap,
Shetland Mainland
Lying between Hillswick and Esha Ness is a landscape
of spectacular red cliffs, culminating in the Heads of
the Grocken. Offshore are many impressive sea stacks.
Using a long lens helped produce a tightly framed
composition and drew in the distant stacks.

156

P.117 Scotland's true north, The Noup, Unst
Since the human eye generally sees detail in shadows, I am reluctant to photograph anything I know will become a silhouette. However the shape of the Noup was so compelling, and the rocks beyond it so appealing with the setting sun that I made an exception here.

P.119 Better than pasta, seaweed, Hillswick, Shetland
Very flat light revealed the colour and variety of seaweeds well here, and since it was not the weather for views I was grateful to find a subject that worked. When I saw the processed film for the first time I was struck by how delicious raw seaweed could look!

P.120 Soft light dawn, Rackwick, Hoy
Rising at four in the morning I was disappointed to find overcast conditions. Yet the boulders of Rackwick still looked wonderful, even without the benefit of flattering light, and I still felt inspired to photograph.

P.121 Tidal Flow, Rackwick, Hoy
The contrast between water in motion and static rock has long intrigued me, and the sandstone boulders of Rackwick seemed the perfect place to make such a picture. A shutter speed around a second gave enough movement without losing all sense of the water's shape.

P.122 Sunset, St Ninian's Isle tombolo, Shetland
The sandy causeway (tombolo) that leads from the Shetland Mainland to St Ninian's Isle is a popular place with families on a summer day. By evening, all have returned to their lodgings, and the sunset is left to be enjoyed in solitude.

P.123 Villians of Ure, Esha Ness, Shetland
These daunting, dark volcanic cliffs really are breath-taking to behold, but are no picnic to photograph. Without bright sunlight their black rock would be horribly gloomy. With it, contrast is challenging, but managed here using a tight composition framed by a long lens.

P.124 Twilight, St Ninian's Isle, Shetland
The mysterious colours of twilight as day turns to night are for me best seen across water. Here, form is minimised and the quality of light itself becomes the theme of the image.

P.125 Beach pebbles, Fladdabister, Shetland
My fondest memories of childhood are of searching for shells and pebbles on beaches in my native Devon, and in Cornwall. I search for them still, though I rarely remove any from the beach now, just the traces of light they leave on my film.

P.127 The Old Man of Hoy
Perfect light for this most iconic subject of the Orkney Islands would have been late sun breaking through heavy cloud with perhaps a little sea fret to add atmosphere. Having to make do with less than perfect can be frustrating, but the composition at least gave me some satisfaction.

P.128 Into the light, The Old Man of Hoy
No angle I could find on the Old Man of Hoy made it seem elegant; it has a presence of brutal strength rather than grace. Shooting into the light silhouetted the tower, which minimised detail and instead dramatised the setting.

P.129 First Light, Ring of Brodgar
Beautifully sited on a peninsula dividing two sheltered sea lochs, I hoped to photograph the Ring of Brodgar as an authentically coastal ancient monument. Unfortunately it is hard to make out the sea clearly from the angle that best dramatises the stones.

P.131 Seabird colonies, cliffs at St Abb's Head
With my tripod poised precariously on the cliff top, and my camera tipped crazily over the edge I took care with lighting, timing, and the validity of the composition, instead of my safety. Such is the life of a landscape photographer.

P.133 *Sand patterns and oil rigs, Cromarty Firth.*
The contrast between nature and heavy industry is one
I know from Teesside, near to my North Yorkshire
home. My priority is to make the best picture I can,
not to pass judgement; that is the prerogative of the
viewer.

P.135 *Foreshore and fine weather, Duncansby Head.*
Textures and colours in the foreshore would have been
better revealed here by more cloud softening the bright
sunlight. Nevertheless, I was grateful for the clear air
and the strong blues of sea and sky.

P.137 *Tangled rope, pre-dawn, Forvie NNR*
In the cold light before dawn a blue cast was
inevitable, without the intervention of a strong
warming filter. Given the colour of the rope, the
graphic nature of the subject, and my less than warm
feelings for it, I left the image unfiltered.

P.138 *Sandstone cave, Cove Bay*
I was attracted both by the smooth shapes and
textures here, and the sculptural quality of the
light. It was necessary to use a graduated neutral
density filter to balance the exposure, or the
brighter areas near the mouth of the cave would
have burnt out.

P.139 *Pebbles on sandstone pavement, Cove Bay*
I was struck by the notion that a land artist like Andy
Goldsworthy would love this place with its beautiful
raw materials. Yet a landscape photographer must
make any disturbance of nature, such as moving
stones to improve composition, artfully invisible.

P.140 *Pebbles, Cove Bay*
Intimate and familiar themes, such as pebbles by the
shore, make a real creative challenge. I try and
achieve a balance between the particular appeal of
the objects themselves, and the integrity of the
compositional structure.

P.141 *Evening light, Moray Firth, from*
Hopeman shore
A rapidly changing sky and approaching tide
combined to force my hand here, so I adopted a
wide-angle view and aimed for atmosphere.
Given more time, much detail on this shore
would have rewarded a closer look.

P.142 *Dunes, Forvie National Nature Reserve*
A drizzly afternoon gave way to a quite stunning
evening, although without direct sunlight. Forvie covers
such a vast area that finding a sandscape untrodden
by human foot presented no real problem.

P.143 *Four views, one morning, Sands of Forvie*
Combining these four images only occurred to me in
the design process of this book. Each image was
intended to stand alone. Nevertheless, since they were
all shot within a couple of hours of one another this
juxtaposition illustrates the sheer variety Forvie offers.

P.144 *Salmon net, St Cyrus National Nature*
Reserve
Most extraordinarily, this image was made at
midday in midsummer. The quality of light that
day was quite fantastic. A wide view dramatised
the perspective created by the net against the
stormy sky. No filter was needed.

P.145 *looking south, St Cyrus National Nature*
Reserve
A little cast shadow from the clouds help relieve
what would otherwise be a predictable
interpretation from an elevated viewpoint.
Nevertheless this is a fair illustration of a typical
eastern Scottish coastal landscape.

P.147 *Folded cliffs, St Abb's Head*
A relatively long focal length lens helped frame tightly
the strong diagonal lines that clearly suggest these
folded cliffs are made of metamorphic rock.

The chief function of this book is visual; to inspire, delight, remind and (occasionally) provoke is my purpose. Although I have some grasp of geology and a sense of the landscape's ecology I am not a scientist or expert, but rather a passionate observer. The reader in the pursuit of in-depth knowledge will find a wealth of more learned sources elsewhere when it comes to the geology, flora, fauna, and history of Scotland's coast.

In the accumulation of these images I found the Pevensey guides a helpful introduction to the Scottish Islands, and, of course, the British Ordnance Survey 1:50,000 (Landranger) maps are superb planning companions. *The Rough Guide to Scotland* was an excellent source of practical information. But I found myself returning to one book in particular. Hamish Haswell-Smith's *The Scottish Islands* may ostensibly be a guide for yachtsmen, but it is much more than that, giving a concise, authoritative account of Scottish history, geology and wildlife. It is beautifully designed and written, and illustrated with useful maps and fine line drawings. I would whole-heartedly recommend it.

I lost count of the number of ferry journeys I made among the Scottish islands, and I would like to acknowledge Caledonian Macbrayne, who run most of Scotland's island ferry crossings, Northlink ferries, and the little independent ferry services that ply the short crossings, for their safe passage.

Additionally I would like to thank Richard Luxmoore and Jill Harden, and Susan and Natalie on St Kilda, all of The National Trust for Scotland; Steve Burge, Nicky Kime and Ken for paddling with me around Mull; fellow photographers Niall Benvie, Duncan McEwan and David Ward for their suggestions about locations; Colin Prior for the inspiration provided by his work; Piers Burnett for putting his faith in me again with this book; Eddie Ephraums for being a great companion in the Northern Isles and St Kilda, and for his co-operation, guidance, endless patience and wisdom with the design. And finally to Jenny and our children Chloe and Sam who accompanied me in Lewis and Harris, and on Arran, Islay and Iona, and for whom I hope this book will be a beginning when it comes to Scotland, and not an end.

159